Measure for Measure

Measure for Measure: A Guidebook for Evaluating Students' Expository Writing was created by the following team of teachers from Berkshire County, Massachusetts:

Norman C. Najimy, *Project Director*, Pittsfield Public Schools, Pittsfield
Winifred Green, *Project Coordinator*, Pittsfield Regional Education
    Center, Pittsfield
James Ace, Taconic High School, Pittsfield
Kathy Armada, Adams Junior High School, Adams
Richard Benson, South Junior High School, Pittsfield
Lee Brown, Nessacus Middle School, Dalton
Bruno Coughlin, North Junior High School, Pittsfield
Toni Gazzaniga, McCann Regional-Technical Vocational High School,
    North Adams
Karen Gralla, Monument Mountain Regional High School, Great Barrington
Lauretta Guiltinan, Pittsfield High School, Pittsfield
Grace Hutchins, Hibbard School, Pittsfield
Kevin Karn, Gateway Regional High School, Huntington
Marion Kasuba, Berkshire Community College, Pittsfield
Myrna Katz, Adams Middle School, Adams
Ann Kuhn, Russell School, Pittsfield
Michelle Lawler, Gateway Regional High School, Huntington
Patricia Masiero, Crane School, Pittsfield
Eugene McCarron, North Adams Middle School, North Adams
Robert Muzesall, Gateway Regional High School, Huntington
Helen Plunkett, Berkshire Community College, Pittsfield
Richard Salinetti, Lee Public Schools, Lee
Margaret Skowron, Crane School, Pittsfield
Edward Udel, Crosby Junior High School, Pittsfield
Diane Uliana, Gateway Regional High School, Huntington

Measure for Measure

A Guidebook for Evaluating
Students' Expository Writing

Edited by

Norman C. Najimy
Pittsfield Public Schools
Berkshire County, Massachusetts

National Council of Teachers of English
1111 Kenyon Road, Urbana, Illinois 61801

NCTE Editorial Board: Paul T. Bryant, Marilyn Hanf Buckley, Thomas C. Clark, Jane Hornburger, Zora Rashkis, Robert F. Hogan, *ex officio*, Paul O'Dea, *ex officio*

Book Design: Tom Kovacs, interior; Gail Glende Rost, cover

NCTE Stock Number 30976

Published 1981 by the National Council of Teachers of English, 1111 Kenyon Road, Urbana, Illinois 61801

Measure for Measure: A Guidebook for Evaluating Students' Expository Writing is reprinted by permission of the Massachusetts Department of Education, which funded in part its original publication. The content of this publication, points of view, or opinions do not necessarily represent the official view or opinions of either the Massachusetts Department of Education or the National Council of Teachers of English.

Library of Congress Catalog Card Number 81-93322

Contents

Preface

"Hasn't anybody taught these kids anything about writing?" This cry is often echoed by teachers faced with the challenge of evaluating a written assignment—whether it be a research report for social studies, a lab report for science, an essay for English, or a subjective test answer for any subject.

Evaluating students' writing is a challenge; the evaluator is placed in the role of a judge, who must examine the case at hand with knowledge, wisdom, and at least a measure of empathy before pronouncing a verdict. That verdict, if unfavorable to the defendant, should not be punitive but instructional. Its purpose must be to help the student develop skills in the craft of writing, which includes the skills of observing, selecting, organizing, and expressing facts, ideas, and feelings in clear, comprehensible language.

Because there are not fixed standards by which students' expository writing can be graded, evaluation of compositions is a highly subjective process. This guide has, therefore, been developed by a team of teachers of English in elementary, middle, secondary, and postsecondary schools in Berkshire County, Massachusetts. Our intent is to help teachers of all subjects in the difficult task of evaluating students' expository writing in a manner that may lead students to grow in the art and craft of writing.

N. C. N.

Evaluation Techniques

Guidelines for Writing Assignments in Subject-Area Classes

The results of a particular writing assignment often correlate with the kind of prewriting experiences and postwriting expectations that the assignment has stimulated. Problems in writing may frequently be traced to students' uncertainty about the assignment and its purpose, their inadequate knowledge about the subject, their lack of motivation, or their suspicion that no one will really be interested in what they have written. Since the development of writing skills is reinforced through writing activities throughout the schools' curricula, the following guidelines are offered for giving an assignment in expository writing in any subject.

Regard writing as a process that requires

    finding information on the subject;

    focusing on a specific topic;

    selecting details pertinent to the topic;

    organizing information into some logical pattern;

    manipulating sentence structure;

    employing conventions such as spelling, punctuation, and usage.

Prepare students adequately for the writing assignment by

    providing enough information or sources of information;

    anticipating problems students may encounter in the process described above;

    demonstrating some ways of solving these problems;

    providing clear and complete directions;

    expecting students to revise, proofread, and rewrite their papers, and to turn in a finished final copy.

Evaluate students' papers by

commending successes;

explaining how to correct weakness or solve problems.

[See "Commenting to Students about Their Writing" and "Adapting Holistic Scoring to the Classroom," both below.]

Make appropriate use of the finished papers by

duplicating particularly effective papers (or parts thereof) for the class to read;

having some papers read aloud;

displaying some papers on a bulletin board;

publishing papers in a class journal, booklet, or textbook or handbook;

using some selections as materials for further class study on the subject.

Composition is a complex process. Though using these guidelines may seem to impose further work upon the instructor and require some additional time, the investment in instruction and time can return substantial profit in students' development of writing skills and mastery of subject matter.

Criteria for Good Writing

Before scoring students' written compositions, the teacher should have in mind—and should make known to the students—some specific criteria by which to evaluate the writing. This set of criteria is offered as a guide for teachers of all disciplines to use when they evaluate papers students have written in response to an assignment. These criteria should be

modified according to learning levels,

developed to increasing degrees of sophistication as students master writing skills,

considered during the reading and evaluating of students' writing.

While all these criteria are standards for good writing, the emphasis on one or more of them may vary, according to the objectives of the assignment. For one assignment, content may outweigh diction; for another assignment, more emphasis may be placed on diction and order. In neither assignment would the other criteria be ignored.

Content

Does the paper focus on a specific subject?

Does the writer demonstrate knowledge of the subject?

Is the purpose of the paper made evident to the reader?

Are generalizations supported by specific details?

Are ideas original and clear or are borrowed ideas credited to their sources?

Organization

Does the introduction prepare the reader for the content?

Is the organization easy to follow?

Is there a clear connection from one point to another?

Are all details related to the purpose of the paper?

Does the conclusion reemphasize the purpose or summarize the content?

Diction

Are words used accurately?

Where appropriate, do words appeal to the reader's senses?

Is the language appropriate to the purpose of the paper and to the intended reader?

Sentence Structure

Are sentences complete?

Are sentences separated by end punctuation?

Are sentences free of choppy, unnecessarily repetitive constructions?

Is sentence structure varied?

Form

Is penmanship legible?

Is the writing free of errors in word usage?

Are words spelled correctly?

Are punctuation marks and capital letters correctly used?

Evaluation: A Step in the Writing Process

No matter how stimulating and creative the writing assignment may be, no matter how much prewriting activity may be involved, the evaluation of students' writing remains a vital step in teaching students how to articulate their observations, feelings, knowledge, and reasoning. Before taking on the responsibility of evaluating compositions—whether they be essays or reports, process papers or test answers—we should make certain assumptions:

If we have given a writing assignment, we have a responsibility to evaluate the writing.

Evaluation of writing is a possible task.

Evaluation involves both subjective and objective aspects.

Evaluation should get to the heart of the writing—content and expression—and not merely to the conventions—punctuation, capitalization, and spelling.

Evaluation should lead to action—revision, reteaching, or reinforcement of successes, and certainly to future improvement.

Thoughtful evaluation of students' writing is evidence of concern for students.

If evaluation is to be honest, realistic, and constructive, perhaps we should ourselves occasionally perform the writing assignment we set for the students. It is one thing to talk about writing, quite another to understand the work and frustration that underlie the act of writing. The writing experience can help us to evaluate students' writing not only as teachers but as writers. As we evaluate, we should keep the following guidelines in mind:

Be aware of the tone of our comments. Writers are defensive about their writing. [See "Commenting to Students about Their Writing," below.]

Give a reason for suggesting stylistic changes. It is more constructive to say "reverse the order of details (or of this sentence) for better emphasis" than to write "weak order" or "vary sentences" or "better to say. . . ."

In the terminal notes, make specific commendations first. Students learn from their successes as well as from their mistakes. Instead of writing "good paragraph," write "you develop the idea with three strong examples."

Use a standard set of symbols to indicate mechanical and technical errors. Allow class time to check the item in a handbook and to correct the error on the paper. [See "Using Correction Symbols," below.]

If a paper is poorly organized, consider making or starting an outline for the student, or asking the student to try outlining the paper as it is written.

Follow up your evaluation. Check to see that the student makes use of your corrections and comments, either by revising the work or by applying the corrections and comments to a subsequent assignment.

Relative Emphasis: Evaluating Content, Form, and Mechanics

The papers have been collected, and they are yours to evaluate. What does a teacher need to know, to weigh, to do? Here is where all teachers who assign writing must shine, for what is written on a students's paper must be carefully considered. Will the comments urge the student to continue to write? Will they evoke a desire to write better? Will the lines of communication be open between teacher and student, or will teacher purpose and student understanding grow apart? What do teachers do with writing that says nothing in a technically correct manner, or with a paper that is solid in content but weak in conventions?

The list of criteria for good writing may suggest a hierarchy of importance, from content to form. Another view is that one criterion can be emphasized for one assignment, and different criteria for other assignments. It is possible that problems in clarity or unity need so much attention that correction of errors in punctuation may be postponed until the more serious problems are solved. If there is a commonality that all teachers should maintain—regardless of how the criteria are used—it is that evaluation must be based on one or more of the criteria and it must be designed to help students to write well.

Before applying the criteria, the teacher must be clear on the nature of the assignment, the prewriting steps, the instructional objectives, and the ability of each student. [See "Guidelines for Writing Assignments in Subject-Area Classes," above.] It is particularly important to keep in mind that any comments, suggestions, directions, or grades be given in proportion to the student's ability to use them to improve writing competency.

It is probable that most papers, after having been evaluated, can be improved by some degree of rewriting. If an entire paper seems to require more effort than a student can probably give, a paragraph, a specific weakness, or a page may be selected to be revised. Spelling can be corrected without rewriting an entire paper. Indeed, if errors are indicated in pencil, it is possible for the students to make corrections before submitting their papers for final evaluation. On the other hand, if a paper is incoherent but contains the seed of an idea, it is a waste of time to correct errors; the effort should be placed on helping the student to cultivate the seed.

In summary, the teacher's creativity and concern should guide the relative emphasis in evaluating each student's work.

Holistic Scoring: An Overview

Holistic scoring is based on the idea that the whole composition is greater than its components, that no components may be judged apart from the whole, and that all components should be judged simultaneously. The term *holistic* derives from *whole*. Holistic scoring, therefore, involves reading and scoring a paper on the total effect of the first impression. In one case, clarity, forcefulness of expression, and originality may outweigh errors in punctuation, spelling, and grammar to create a positive impression. In another case, errors in syntax or mechanics may predominate to the point of obscuring the meaning and producing a negative impression of the paper.

Holistic scoring involves a team approach. Scorers first read and analyze the topic on which a set of papers has been written. They then read and discuss a sample of those papers and establish some standards by which the particular set of compositions may be scored "superior," "good," "fair," or "poor." They then proceed with the scoring process for the entire set of papers.

Each paper is read by two or three evaluators, who independently score the paper on a four-point scale ranging from superior (4) to poor (1). (So that one reader does not know how another reader has scored a paper, each reader may be assigned a different code to stand for 4, 3, 2, 1, or the readers may mark their scores on separate lists of a class set.) If the scores on a paper are adjacent on the numerical scale (for example, 1/2, 2/3, 3/4) or identical, they are added to give a total. If they vary more widely (for example, 1/3, 2/4, 1/4), another reader—usually a person who has been appointed chief reader—decides how the paper should be scored.

Advantages of holistic scoring are numerous. The process is efficient, for it requires that less time be spent on each paper. It requires consensus among the scorers; indeed, when scores vary widely, worthwhile discussion usually ensues regarding the merits of the paper and what constitutes good writing. It usually stresses positive aspects of students' writing. It involves scorers (teachers of writing) in articulating a set of standards to guide their determination of a paper's score.

Holistic scoring, unlike analytical scoring, does not provide for the correction of errors and the writing of comments to writers regarding their compositions. It is, however, a valid way of scoring large sets of compositions.

Adapting Holistic Scoring to the Classroom

Engaging students in holistic scoring of papers written by students on a given topic can be dually beneficial. The students become increasingly aware of what makes a good expository paragraph—the kind they will need to write when they answer subjective test questions. Also, they closely examine the subject matter and so reinforce what they know or learn something that they did not know.

The process is not difficult. On one day, give students a specific topic on which they should write no more than one page—or as little as one paragraph. The topic should be drawn from recent or current class study and should be limited enough to allow students to address the topic within fifteen or twenty minutes. For example:

1. Explain what a food chain is. Give a specific example that illustrates your explanation.
2. An ideal of youth in Ancient Greece was to be physically strong and mentally alert. Show how one of the heroes we have studied exemplifies this ideal.
3. Describe how one of the cultural groups we have studied has adapted to the climate in which it lives. Be sure to identify the group and the type of climate.
4. In the play *Julius Caesar*, a soldier thinks of Caesar as an eagle. Cassius considers him a wolf, and Brutus suggests that he's a snake in its shell. Explain what each person means by the metaphor he uses.

The teacher should also write a response to the topic in order to know more precisely what a response should include and to discover any problems that the item may cause.

After allowing about fifteen to twenty minutes for the writing of the papers, collect them. Score them holistically, using a scale of 1 (poor), 2 (fair), 3 (good), 4 (excellent). Place the number on the back of the student's paper. From the 2-3-4 papers, choose three or four, taking at least one from each score. (There is little value in having the class examine a paper scored 1.) Blank out the students' names and duplicate those papers, making a copy for each student in the class.

At the next class meeting, distribute the duplicated papers and ask the students to read and score each paper on the 1-2-3-4 scale. Allow no more than ten minutes for scoring the papers. Then hold a discussion of the papers—their accuracy, clarity, organization, relevance to the topic, and so on. Survey the degree of consensus of scores assigned by the students to each paper. Reexamine any paper on which there seems to be wide discrepancy of scores.

It is this discussion that leads to greater understanding of what good expository writing is, and to increased knowledge of the subject matter being taught. The entire activity, including the writing, holistic scoring by students, and the discussion, takes about half of each of two class periods.

Holistic Scoring as a Prerevision Step

Holistic scoring by students is a valuable way of teaching revision of composition. After students have written a readable draft of a composition, ask them to use their telephone numbers (or some other code) in place of their names and collect their papers. Then divide the class into groups of three or four. Next, give each group a number of compositions equal to the number of students in the group. Be sure that no group receives papers written by anyone in that group. Give each student a strip of paper on which to record the code numbers of all three or four papers given that group. Each student in the group should read each paper, evaluate it on a 4-3-2-1 scale (using criteria established during prewriting activities), and place the score for each paper opposite the code listed on the strip of paper. Then each student passes the paper to the next person in the group, until all members of the group have read and scored the three or four papers given to them. Finally, the students compare the scores they have assigned to each paper and discuss reasons for the scores.

Two options may follow this activity. One is that the teacher may place a five-column chart on the board, the first labeled "Paper No." and the rest labeled "4-3-2-1." The scores are then recorded on the chart, to show the degree of agreement or discrepancy of judgment among the readers. Another option is that each group may write a short note of praise or constructive criticism to attach to each paper scored by that group.

Finally, papers are returned to their authors for revision. This holistic scoring prior to revision takes about half an hour and pays dividends that make the investment a profitable one for both the students and the teacher.

Analytical Scoring: An Overview

What is the difference between analytical and holistic scoring? Analytical scoring of students' papers involves the close reading and examination of the many components of each paper—the content, organization, sentence structure, punctuation, spelling, and so on. We score analytically when we mark spelling errors, insert punctuation marks, call attention to need for transitional phrases, correct an error in agreement, or point out that an idea is too vague, an expression is trite, or a paragraph is disorganized.

Before scoring papers analytically the evaluator establishes specific criteria by which the papers will be judged:

Does this paper contain certain points of information?

Is it organized according to a certain pattern?

Is it free of errors in x, y, and z?

Does it fulfill the purpose (to _____)?

Criteria for evaluating a set of papers analytically may be selected from those listed under "Criteria for Good Writing," above.

Analytical scoring provides opportunities for teachers to help students develop the craft of writing. It allows the evaluator to describe a paper's strengths and weaknesses for the writer, point out errors or make corrections, comment on the quality of a paper, or make suggestions for improving it. It also offers opportunities for teacher and student to focus on specific problems in writing that need attention, for by analyzing the paper, the teacher can prescribe a remedy for a certain ailment.

Analytical scoring has some disadvantages. It is time-consuming because it calls for careful examination of a paper. Sometimes this examination focuses the reader's attention on flaws, so that the papers's total effect may be subordinated to consideration of its parts. Unless the evaluator's comments are constructive, analytical scoring can have the negative effects of stressing only the flaws and of convincing students that writing is a punitive activity leading to failure. For suggestions on how to make analytical scoring a constructive, productive effort, see "Evaluation: A Step in the Writing Process," above, and "Commenting to Students about Their Writing," below.

Considered and treated as a step in teaching the writing process, analytical scoring of students' writing is an important contribution to developing the craft of writing. It can be worth the work.

Analytical and Holistic Scoring: Advantages, Disadvantages

Analytical Scoring

> Precise criteria make decisions concerning correctness relatively easy.

> Identification of particular components (or skills) that an individual needs to work on is facilitated.

> The scorer may address specific comments about a particular composition to the writer of that paper.

> Analysis of components of a composition is time-consuming.

> Using a standard set of criteria for evaluating all papers may be over-restrictive.

> Scoring is done by one evaluator, so no opportunity is offered to scorers to gain new insights through prescoring sessions.

> Emphasis is often placed on flaws rather than strengths of a paper.

Holistic Scoring

> Criteria treat writing as a whole product, rather than as a set of separate components. The components are therefore considered simultaneously.

> Having more than one evaluator score each paper leads to a fairly accurate assessment of a student's overall writing ability.

During the prescoring sessions, evaluators have opportunities to gain new insights into writing through discussion of strengths and weaknesses of sample papers, and through sharing of ideas about writing. These insights often carry over into classroom teaching practices.

Emphasis is usally placed on strengths of a paper.

Many papers may be read and scored in relatively short time.

There is no opportunity for an evaluator to address specific comments about a particular composition to the writer.

[Adapted from *Basic Skills Assessment: Manual for Scoring the Writing Sample*, published by Educational Testing Service.]

Using Correction Symbols

Grammar, punctuation, capitalization, and spelling do not in themselves constitute the highest skills of the writing process. Nevertheless, students need to master the conventions because readers expect writers to use them—and because these conventions do indeed contribute to effective written communication. When analytically evaluating students' papers, the teacher needs to address problems in mechanics of the writing.

The use of a standard set of correction symbols is not meant to focus on the conventions of writing more than on the content, language, and organization. It is meant instead to prevent confusion about what the symbols mean. The use of a standard set of correction symbols from grade to grade and across all subject disciplines in which the students write should familiarize students with the meaning of the symbols.

When using these symbols, a teacher must consider the current needs of the student. The choice of corrections made by the teacher should depend on the student's grade level, ability, and knowledge. For example, to use a symbol signifying lack of parallelism on a paper written by a student who does not understand the principle of parallel structure is likely to be a futile gesture on the part of the teacher and meaningless for the student. If a student is incapable of finding the correct spelling of *pneumatic* or *gnu*, it may be more productive to spell the word correctly for the student than to use a symbol.

The most effective way for a teacher to use these symbols is to select those most relevant to the class. Then, in the beginning of the year, the teacher should explain the symbols, give examples of the error each symbol signifies, and demonstrate ways to avoid or correct those errors. Ideally, the teacher will reinforce recognition and correction of the errors by having students edit their papers and present corrected copies.

The symbols included here do not represent every kind of error in grammar, usage, spelling, or punctuation. The set is deliberately limited. While teachers of rhetoric or advanced composition may wish to add symbols, this set is designed to address common errors and to be manageable for students' use. The following explanation of symbols may be duplicated and distributed to students. They should be given time to examine the explanation of the symbols before making corrections when their papers are returned for revision.

Correction Symbols and Their Explanations

To the student: You've been handed back your composition. The thought and energy and hard work that you've put into it are paid off with scrawls and squiggles that indicate you've done something wrong—but you're not quite sure what you've done wrong, or how to do it right. Here is a list of some commonly used symbols, with an explanation of the error that each symbol stands for, and some suggested ways to correct the error. As you work on solving each problem, you may find fewer symbols per page with each composition you write in the future.

Problems with Words

   sp *Spelling*: A word is spelled wrong. Consult a dictionary or a spelling book, or see if your teacher has given you the correct spelling.

   T *Tense*: The tense of the verb is incorrect. Perhaps you started to use the past tense and then, for no reason, shifted to the present.

Example: I was minding my own business. A cold hand grasps my wrist.

Solution: I was minding my own business. A cold hand grasped my wrist.

Consult an English text. Look up "verbs-tense" or "consistency of tense."

D *Diction*: You may have used a vague word (such as *said* or *house*) where a more specific word (such as *shouted* or *hovel*) would be more effective.

ww *Wrong word*: You have used a word incorrectly.

Examples: They were *overtaken* by smoke. / The students studied very hard for *there* test. / After sending them out of the room, the teacher *revoked* them.

Look up the word in a dictionary, consult the homonym section of an English book. If these don't help, ask your teacher.

∧ *Omission*: A word or phrase is needed to make the sentence clear.

u *Usage*: The wrong form of a word is used, as in these sentences: *Her* and *me* were chosen. / I did *good* on the test. / They *snuk* up on us.

Problems with Sentences

RO *Run-on sentence*: Two sentences are punctuated as one. Read the sentence aloud. Place the appropriate end-punctuation (period, question mark, or exclamation mark) where it belongs or use connecting words.

Example: It was the last day of school even the principal was happy.
Solutions: It was the last day of school. Even the principal was happy. / It was the last day of school, and even the principal was happy. / Because it was the last day of school, even the principal was happy.

F *Fragment*: The group of words is not a sentence.

Example: Because I wasn't sure of the answer.
Solution: I wasn't sure of the answer. Because I wasn't sure of the answer I left it blank.

dang *Dangling phrase*: A phrase does not modify the word it is meant to.

Example: Turning the corner, the mountain came into view.
Solutions: Turning the corner, we could see the mountain. / As we turned the corner, the mountain came into view.

Consult an English text. Look up "participial phrases—dangling."

agr *Agreement*: A verb and its subject do not agree in number; either the verb is singular and the subject is plural or vice versa.

Example: Every person in the bleachers are waving a banner.
Solutions: Every person in the bleachers is waving a banner. / All the people in the bleachers are waving banners.

This symbol may also mean that a pronoun does not agree in number with the noun it refers to; one is singular, the other is plural.

Example: No serf of feudal lords owned their own house.
Solutions: No serf of feudal lords owned his or her own house. / No serfs of feudal lords owned their own houses.

Consult an English text. Look up "agreement."

P *Pronoun reference*: The noun that a pronoun refers to is not clear.

Example: When the Spitfires met the Daredevils, they challenged them.
Solution: The Daredevils challenged the Spitfires when the two gangs met.
Example: Other gangs know that the Spitfires are fearless, and they respect them.
Solution: Other gangs respect the Spitfires' fearlessness.

Consult an English text. Look up "pronoun-reference" or "antecedent."

? *Unclear*: The meaning of a sentence is not clear to a reader. Reread the sentence. Then rewrite it.

Problems with Paragraphs

¶ *Start a new paragraph here*: Because you have started a new topic, or a new unit of related details, you should start a new paragraph.

No ¶ *Do not start a new paragraph*: Since you are continuing with the same set of related ideas, there is no need to start a new paragraph.

SS *Subject shift*: You started writing in one person, then shifted to another. Use the same person.

Example: One of my most satisfying activities is cross-country skiing. When you get into the snow-filled woods, your nerves relax and you find peace.

Solution: One of my most satisfying activities is cross-country skiing. When I get into the woods, my nerves relax, and I find peace.

Consult an English text. Look up "subject shift."

Rep *Repetitive* (or *redundant*): Either the same information is unnecessarily repeated or a certain word or phrase is unnecessary because it means the same as another word or phrase in the passage.

Example: In this modern society of today, people seem to be rushing about quickly and aimlessly. Many don't know where they are going.

Solution: In this modern society many people seem to be rushing about aimlessly. These people need to pause and ask, "Where am I going?"

Problems with Punctuation

○ *Punctuation mark omitted*: Some punctuation mark is needed here.

Example: The children's program begins at 2:30 p.m.
Solution: The children's program begins at 2:30 p.m.

∅ *Punctuation mark is incorrect or unnecessary*: The punctuation mark should be removed.

Example: The children's program begins at 2:30 p.m.
Solution: The children's program begins at 2:30 p.m.

Commenting to Students about Their Writing

Teachers who assign written composition in any discipline should subscribe to a philosophy that evaluation of writing is an important step in helping students develop the craft of writing. This philosophy is evidenced in the manner in which we speak to students about their writing.

It is not enough simply to put a grade and some corrections on a student's piece of writing. More important than grades or corrections is what we teachers say to students about their writing—and how we say it. Our comments must be designed to help students develop the craft of writing. [See "Guidelines for Giving Writing Assignments in Subject-Area Classes," above.] When writing comments to a student about a paper, we must be considerate of that student's strengths and weaknesses and then write comments that will reinforce those strengths and address those weaknesses.

Students respond more positively to constructive, personalized comments than they do to negative criticism. Terms such as *dull, trite, vague,* or *irrelevant,* or comments such as "It's obvious that you scrawled this out at the last minute" often make students feel discouraged about their ability to write. Such comments, especially when tendered without concrete suggestions, confirm students' convictions that writing is a punitive act.

From elementary grades through high school and beyond, many students need to be assured that writing is a creative process, which they are capable of performing. To establish and reinforce students' convictions that they can learn to write, wise teachers start with a positive point: "You really help me to see." "Your directions are easy to follow." "Your first argument is a strong one." "Great phrase!" It is important to alert students to something they've done right, as well as to point out something they've done wrong. It is vital to explain how to remedy a problem, rather than simply to state that there is a problem.

Criticism is made constructive by suggesting ways to improve the paper. Constructive criticism narrows the criticism to a specific problem, helps the student to understand the problem, and suggests how the problem may be solved. Constructive comments can help students to develop positive attitudes toward writing, assuring students that they can write, and that they can express what they know, think, need, or feel, in clearly written composition.

Examples of Constructive Comments

This section suggests some ways to comment to students about their writing so that we not only alert students to a problem but also help them to understand and solve that problem. While these suggestions do not cover the entire range of possible problems we encounter as we evaluate students' writing, they do offer examples of appropriate tone and specificity which can characterize our notes to students about their compositions. The comments in italic are vague and not particularly helpful. The alternative examples that follow are constructive in tone and specificity.

> *Irrelevant—this has nothing to do with your topic.*

>> This fact is true. You need to relate it to your topic by explaining how it affects (the food chain) (Brutus's decision) (the need for a new law).

How is this detail (that polar bears are a main attraction at the zoo) related to your purpose (to show how an animal is adapted to its environment)?

Your final paragraph starts a new topic. Revise it (to summarize the details in the body of your paper) (to emphasize that the evidence you have given supports your theory) (to underscore that each side's insistence that it is totally right may cause another war).

This information can be the topic of another paper. Save it! Since you are trying to describe the Valentine displays at the candy store, you should not discuss the effects of candy on teeth. Instead, try to show more of the colors, shapes, and smells of the displays.

To show your readers that you've shifted to the past, use a phrase here such as (The whistle reminded me of . . .) (Last month . . .) (It hasn't always been . . .).

Your paper is full of vague, general statements which you do not support.

Make a list of specific (examples) (facts) (incidents) (word pictures) that (support) (prove) (demonstrate) (illustrate) this statement. Then choose three or four of these to develop your paragraph.

You say that chopping wood is hard work. Show that it is by describing the weight of the axe, the vibration of the blows, the feelings in your arm and back.

To demonstrate how the Tories and the Whigs differed, explain each group's position on some specific issues, such as the Stamp Tax, British troops in Boston, and the Port of Boston Act.

Your opening line grabs attention. Carry the idea through by identifying and describing some life-forms that flourish under rocks—such as centipedes, sow bugs, and worms.

You need to prove that Godfrey is a hypocrite. Point out specific contradictions between what he pretends to be and what he hides.

Can you help us to see your dog?

Try to show us you were afraid without using the words *fear, afraid, scary, scared,* or *frightened.* Instead, describe what you saw, what you heard, what you did, and what happened to you.

Your mention of the effects of candy on the teeth can be made relevant by including the idea that, in spite of these effects, ...

Your details are so disorganized that they confuse the reader.

List the steps for (changing spark plugs) (playing backgammon) (taking 35 mm slides) (making candles) in order. Use terms such as *first, while, be sure to, next,* and *after* to connect these steps. Then describe the steps in order.

Pretend you are shooting a film of the scene. Decide where you will begin, in what direction you will move, what details you will focus on, and where you will end. Use that pattern to organize your description.

Since this is your strongest argument, place it last. As the climax of your essay, it will make a stronger impression on readers.

Details are specific and clear. They need to be organized so that a reader who does not know the topic can follow your comparison. Try one of these patterns:

Introduction	Introduction	
Rock and Swing	Rock	Swing
Major Instruments	Instruments	Instruments
Most Common Rhythms	Rhythms	Rhythms
Themes of Lyrics	Themes	Themes
Moods Created	Effects on	Effects on
	Listeners	Listeners
Conclusion	Conclusion	

Redundant or Repetitive. You keep saying the same thing over again.

Combine these sentences into one so that the underlined words need not be repeated.

Instead of repeating that (school is like a prison) (a system of bicycle trails should be built) (everything had changed in Tarrytown) explain what you mean. (What rules, physical features, and activities make school like a prison?) (Show where the trails should be built, how they could be paid for, who would use them, and how the trails would help people.) (What specific changes did Rip observe when he returned to Tarrytown?)

Reread this sentence aloud. What phrase can be cut?

Four times you tell us that (the Berkshires is a great place to live) (goldfish make fine pets) (the United States was the aggressor in the Mexican-American War) (radials are better than bias-ply tires). Make the statement only once. Then prove it with specific reasons. (Cite recreational opportunities or scenery or culture.) (Describe the calming effects of observing goldfish.) (Explain the role of Manifest Destiny.) (Tell how long radials last or how much they improve gas mileage.)

Applications with Examples

This brief portfolio of papers offers some examples of how teachers have applied ideas and techniques described in this booklet. The editor intends the sampling to represent many grades and a variety of topics.

Four Papers and Their Evaluations

Paper one: Fourth-grader S_____ had a story to tell. She wrote unhesitatingly. On the next page is part of the result. Discouraging? Yes. Hopeless? No! In that increasingly incoherent jumble, the teacher knew there was a message. Starting to correct the errors, the teacher soon realized that there would be nearly as many corrections as there were words in the story.

The teacher asked S_____ to read her story, while the teacher observed the writing and, on separate paper, took a few verbatim notes to record phrases that were not decipherable from the writing. Then the teacher copied S_____'s story, with words spelled correctly and punctuation marks and capital letters in their places.

S_____ was given the story she wrote, copied as it should be. She was asked to recopy the model, so that it could be shared—in her handwriting—with other people. To help her with the recopying, she was given a 6" x 9" card to use as a marker and a dot was placed at the starting point of each line on the paper.

The story does not end there. Like her classmates, the writer designed her own book, recopied her story in her own illustrated format, and, before an audience of little children and adults, read her story aloud. S_____, who rarely knew the joy of success, thoroughly enjoyed the audience's attention and applause.

This success helped S_____ to dispel the notion that she could never learn how to write and it gave her teachers a starting point from which to teach her.

21

All about the Boinic Bird

One day two owls said, "Help me, help me!" said the one owl. The eagle came to eat me he said to the owl no one is near everone is miles and miles and miles a way. you have to lat me can't you and eas boat elxse no you are big and plumped can find someone for you to eat "like a worm. help me help me Herman help me Herman his sitter said Herman she knocked and knocked on his door she opened the slowly and slowly then she saw him on the floor she thet he fell a sleep but he was not a sleep he was pooked out whil a harman he cadine help yet becuas he was mocked out and I said to him whack up he hey he comt whack up what cam I do he as ratyt to eat him Will call area mother mother mother the agel is aug to eat jorne we cant save him and the huaman has den trucks it how can we save him mother mother What happy happen brother must all

From the revised version:

One day an owl said, "Help me! The eagle has come to eat me!" The eagle said to the owl, "No one is near. everyone is miles and miles away." "Do you have to Eat me? can't you find anybody else?" "No, you are a big plump owl." "I can find someone for you to eat, like a worm. Help me! Help me! Herman!"

Paper two: The assignment for this paper asked the student to describe the benefits of reading a biography of the student's choice.

Ther were many benefits in this biography. First, there was Maia's want for her country to win the war. She and her brother steal ammunition from the Germans to shoot them when they go on parade. The reader benefited from this by learning that, even if a situation seemed desparate, one can still try to help. Another benefit was Maia's ability to learn many languages without the benefit of school. This was good because it showed that if a person is determined enough, they can learn to do just about anything, even if it seems impossible. The most important benefit was Maia's love for her father. Even though he neglected the family and tried to get away form them, especially when he was not allowed to fight, Maia forgave him and continued to love and admire him. Maia's devotion to her country, her ability to learn, and her love for her father were some of the reasons why this autobiography was a great book to the reader.

The student's paper received the following comments from the teacher.

1. As a noun, *want* means "lack of." In this case use "desire that her country . . . ."
2. Perhaps you mean, "I benefited from reading about Maia's love . . . ."
3. Revise this sentence to tell how her love for her father affected you.
4. Your concluding sentence is clear and concise. Good!

   N _____, in your opening you should identify the title and the author. Change verbs mark *T* to simple present, because the book is still in existence.

   I like your arrangement of details in order of importance.

Some further considerations seem pertinent to the evaluation of this paper. Giving a topic is an effective way to limit the focus of a paper, but the word *benefit* in this assignment could be confusing. Perhaps a rephrasing of the topic sentence would help this student, for example, "I learned a great deal from reading _____." Also, students should be asked to supply the title of the book and the name of the author.

Paper three: This paper was written in response to the same assignment as paper two.

> Many benefits cam from reading this book' First of all, Knight shows the great devotion on a dog to its master. Lassie traveled over four hundred miles just to meet Joe at the school gate. Although not all dogs travel this far, many embark on incredible ① journeys to be reunited with their masters. Knight also shows that no matter how tame one may think their dog may be, the dog still has natral instincts on their ancestors. Lassie always relied on humans for food, water, and shelter. But she had to hunt and find her own shelter during her journey relying on ② her instincts. Most important, though, is the courageous honesty displayed by Carracloughs. Although they had many chances to keep Lassie while she was rightfully the Duke's they did not, and were ready to return her after he four hundred mile journey home.

This student's paper received the following teacher's comments.

> N_____, you clearly summarize some points in the story. You do not explain how reading the book benefited you.
> Did you learn anything about relationships between people and pets?
> Has the story changed any ideas you had about animals or attitudes toward them?
> 1. Fine sentence! You've used mature words well and emphasized an unusual fact.
> 2. Good example.
> Check and correct errors in agreement of pronouns.

This paper also suffers from weak direction, for the word *benefits* seems not to have been made clear. The student has made a good selection of points to be admired in the story, but has not used them to support the topic sentence. The details trail off without reaching any conclusion.

Paper four: One further example paper with teacher's comments. The student seems to have defined the assignment for himself.

(1) I worked for an auto parts store for a year and eight months. I did the same thing every day. I would get their at eight o'clock every morning and punch my card. First I would check in the shipment and then put it away. Then I would collect all the cores (old starters, water pumps, fuel pumps, clutches, and distributors). I would tag them and then throw in the core barrels. When I got done with the cores I usually went up and down the isles picking up merchandise that had fallen from the shelves. I was the one that always had to do this. The counter workers wouldn't even think of it. They would drop something on the floor and leave it their. They would say to themselves, "Thats OK Joe will pick it up." I hated it when they did this. At the end of the day I would sweep and mop the floors. I don't know why I had to do this. The tile on the floor was old it looked better when it wasn't mopped. At this time it was five o'clock. I would punch my card and leave the store immediately. I finally quit that job and (2) as I look on it the prices were totally outragous. At one time when I was their a gallon of anti-freeze costs $7.00. The store would only pay $3.00. A gallon of wind shield washer solvent costs (3) the customers 1.99 a gallon, the store would pay only .89. Starters and alternators are very expensive. The store would sell them to customers for almost twice their costs. Now as I look cack at my job I felt like a customer. They would raise the prices and think very little of me because I had to pay the prices for working their.

This paper received the following comments.

J_____ , your detailing of the job routine and of how you were treated shows the boredom of the job and suggests the need for people to work at a job they can like.

1. Good explanation.
2. End your paper here.
3. This is another topic. You may want to write another paragraph on price-gouging. Be sure, though, to get correct information.

Use *there–here–where* to refer to *place*.

Use *their* as a possessive: *their friends, their places*.

isles = islands
aisles = rows

Evaluation and Revision: Two Examples

Since evaluation is but a step in the writing process, an evaluation should lead to action. The following are examples of one kind of action: revision based on suggestions made through constructive comments.

Paper one: This is the student's first draft. **①**

During the summer season, Wellfleet displays the hustle and bustle of vacation life, but when winter comes everything seems to slow down. Wellfleet is considered a vacation town where many people spend time during the summer. When winter comes, however, the only people that can be found are the residents or **②** natives of the town. The population drops rapidly from about twenty thousand in the summer to less than one thousand in the winter.

The sand dunes don't noticeably change from season to season, **③** but do change from year to year. It is beautiful at the beach when the sun is shining and there is a slight breeze. Many people may be found refreshing themselves in the cooling water of the Atlantic **④** Ocean. But as soon as the temperature drops, the beach becomes evacuated and the waves which people row in on are now rough and choppy. **①**

Summer, being the in-season, every restaurant, boutique and supermarket is open. While in the off-season, a few restaurants and supermarkets are open, but no boutique or gift shops.

Both pleasure and fishing boats fill the marina in the summer, making it difficult to find a spot to dock. Buring the winter, the only boats to be found are commercial fishing boats which bring in the lobster and fish supply.

The ponds freeze over in the winter covering up the place where many families used to swim. Ice skaters can now be found gliding around the ponds. All year long the air in Wellfleet is clean **⑤** because there is no industry in town.

⑥ Our house never changes from summer to winter. It is always feaceful and relaxing because it is away from sity life. The land around the house changes from green leaves in the summer to **⑦** barren trees in the winter.

Wellfleet is a much more active town in the summer than in the winter. The population drop every winter shows this. Even though most things are closed in winter, Wellfleet still is a cozy little town.   **⑧**

The first draft received the following comments aimed at guiding the student in his revision.

> Randi-Knowing Wellfleet, I enjoyed reading your paper; it stirred up many pleasant memories.
>
> Since you know and love the town so well, here are a few suggestions that might help make your comparison even more vigorous. For openers, how about a title? Remember all essays have titles.
>
> 1. Here, express your idea more naturally—Wellfleet doesn't "display hustle and bustle." *Filled* may be an ordinary word but it does the job here. People *leave* the beach; it is not "evacuated." Remember Strunk and White's admonition about preferring the natural to the elegant or strained expression.
> 2. Isn't all this repetition of sentence one? Why not give specific details of these differences?
> 3. Could you clarify this?
> 4. Here you have another excellent source of contrast. Use specific details to liven it up.
> 5. An interesting detail, but how does it relate to your purpose?
> 6. Connect the cottage to Wellfleet in paragraph one, or else this will sound like a new topic.
> 7. The *land* changes this way? Are you saying precisely what you mean?
> 8. This (like no. 6 above) suggests an emphasis not developed in your paper. Stick to the thesis.
>
> Please revise. Who knows? Maybe we can sell your essay to the Cape Cod Chamber of Commerce!

Randi revised his essay as follows.

Wellfleet

Wellfleet, the small Cape Cod town where my family has a summer cottage, is vastly different in winter from the exciting community I know so well. In summer every street and beach is alive with the hustle and bustle of tourists. In restaurants, boutiques and the supermarkets, business thrives. When winter comes, however, only the local townspeople trudge through snowswept streets. Boutiques and gift shops are boarded up, and only the supermarket remains open. The population drops rapidly from twenty thousand to fewer than a thousand.

At the beach the sand dunes themselves don't change from season to season, but the view over them certainly does. In the light summer breeze the sun shines on multi-colored sun umbrellas dotting the beach. The laughter and shrill cries of children dashing back and forth from the water to their sand castles filter into the sounds of Red Sox games and the lively rock music from portable radios beside the striped beach chairs. Hundreds splash around in the cooling waters of the Atlantic. But in the frigid days of winter the lonely shriek of the wind swirls over the empty dunes. Only an occasional gull or the bent form of an individual walking into the wind or throwing a shell into the waves breaks the monotony—those same waves where last summer young people on surf boards rode the crests.

Both pleasure and fishing boats fill the marina in the summer, making it difficult to find a spot at the dock. During the winter, the only boats to be found are commercial fishing boats which bring in the lobster and fish supply.

To be sure, Wellfleet in winter differs greatly from Wellfleet in summer, but regardless of the season, our cottage in this lovely seaside town is a warm, cozy place filled with memories of both seasons.

The successful revision received the following praise from the teacher.

Randi-Your revised description paints vivid comparisons. Details in the second paragraph really appeal to the readers' eyes and ears. Your concluding paragraph is an appropriate reflection on the scenes you've painted. Why not send it to the Wellfleet officials?

Paper two: The assignment for this paper and revision stated:

We often pass by or through a place without opening our eyes and ears to the sights and sounds that place offers us. Take a walk in a place near your home or school. Observe some of the sights and sounds. Then describe what you saw and heard along your walk.

Some of the students who wrote for this assignment created effective sensory descriptions. Others wrote lists of details disjoined from each other and stimulating no single effect. The following first draft exemplifies this problem.

A Walk in the Woods

Friday I took a walk in the woods at the bottom of my street where I live. I stepped on some branches and they cracked. The noise aroused wildlife around me. I slumped over to pick up a leave and I scuffed my foot on a rock. I went on and I came to a spring with clean water spring water. I stopped for a while to get a drink. I looked at the railroad tracks that went by the woods a train raced by. The noise was terrible. It echoed through the woods. The noise rang in my ears and the steel wheels were clanging on the rails. The sky was now getting dark, so I walked home. On my way I saw a battered up car. I finally made it home. I slumped into our padded reclining chair and rested. I was a casualty of exaustion.

The following comments of the evaluator helped the student to establish a focus and to create a clearer word-picture.

1. Give some specific examples. Show, don't just tell us that you disturbed wildlife.
2. Why? Did something make you look at them?
3. Good description. I can hear it. Did it last long?
4. How is this related to the woodland scene? If it isn't related, cut it.
5. Your ending is not convincing. The walk does not seem strenuous enough to make you exhausted.
   Larry—You have a situation that can be developed into a vivid picture of how people and their machines intrude upon nature. Try to develop it by *showing* how you and the train disturbed the woods.

Here is Larry's revision:

Intrusion in the Woods

Friday I took a walk in the woods at the bottom of my street. At the entrance I stepped from sun-baked pavement to a soft and cool earth. I stepped on some branches that crackled under me. A startled squirril darted up a pine tree and some birds—chickadees or sparrows—fluttered above me. I bent down to pick up a rust colored leave and scuffed my foot on a rock. The rock rolled down the slight hill, and where it had been I noticed some little bugs, with hair-like legs, scurrying about, maybe looking for shelter. I came to a cool spring and stopped for a while to get a drink of clear water. I felt the earth rumble under my hands and knees. I looked at the railroad tracks that cut through the woods. The train roared closer. Soon the noise of the engine was echoing throughout the woods and ringing in my ears. The steel wheels were clanging on the steel tracks. I pressed my hands onto my ears to muffle the noise. The roar and clang faded away, and I turned homeward. The sky was getting dark. Behind me my forest was at peace.

The revision elicited the following comment.

Larry, your revision works. I can see and hear it.

Allowing Writers Time

Ordering experience requires reflection. Expressing experience
requires time and space to find the right words, to make mistakes,
to discover and record precisely what the writer has experienced.
What follows is a demonstration of how one junior high school
student crafted her essay—and the extent of her effort—to share
one of her poignant experiences. The student was allowed time to
reflect upon the experience and to draft her thoughts, to try words
and phrases, to scratch out and to try again. The result attests to
the worth of allowing the writer time and space.

The student's revised draft:

This story is very hard for me to write But I wanted to share my poignant story with others).

When I was young I was stricken with leukemia but I was lucky enough to ~~live~~ survive after fourteen years of struggling with this killer. although I experienced many days of pain and ~~suffering~~.

Then something beautiful ~~happened~~, My Mother had given birth to a little baby girl at the age of eight mõths she was also stricken with leukemia. To me it was the most odius thing which could ~~have~~ happened. This child ~~helped~~ me look at life from a different angle instead of waking up to grief and sorrow I found myself looking forward to the days shared with my little sister.

When she died I didnt turn away I face it for I had grown alot in the past year. I tried my hardest to make the last of her very short life comfortable for her. Every day I would sit with her, sing with her and on sunny days we would sit together on the front porch watching other children play and watching the great oak trees stand stoical ~~so~~ looking out at the world I realized that the child in my arms would never play with other children or climb that big oak tree Her life had only begun and now it had ended.

All my life I will remember this young small, ~~child~~ beautiful child. For she was my will to live, my reason for joy I knew her for only a short while.

Suggested Readings on Evaluation

Cooper, C. R., and Odell, Lee. *Evaluating Writing: Describing, Measuring, Judging.* Urbana, Ill.: NCTE, 1977.

Diedrich, Paul B. *Measuring Growth in English.* Urbana, Ill.: NCTE, 1974.

Hillard, Helen, ed. *Suggestions for Evaluating Senior High School Writing.* Pittsburg: Association of English Teachers of Western Pennsylvania, 1963.

Judine, Sister M. *Guide for Evaluating Student Composition.* Champaign, Ill.: NCTE, 1965.

Winn, N. F., et al. *A Scale for Evaluation of High School Student Essays.* Champaign, Ill.: NCTE, 1960.

These titles are all available from the National Council of Teachers of English, 1111 Kenyon Road, Urbana, Illinois 61801.